T0106024

HISTORICAL NOTES.

THE earliest known musical celebration of St. Cecilia's Day (November 22) was held at Evereux, in France, in the year 1571. More than a century elapsed, however, before St. Cecilia was similarly honoured in England. For the " Feast," as it was called, in 1683—the first held in this country—three odes were written, two in English and one in Latin. All three were set to music by Henry Purcell, but only one appears to have been publicly performed.

John Dryden (1631-1700) wrote two odes in honour of the patroness of music and musicians—" A Song for St. Cecilia's Day," in 1687, and, in 1697, " Alexander's Feast, or the Power of Music." Both these odes were subsequently set to music by Handel. The text of the first of these, forming that of the present publication, originally appeared printed on a broadside headed :

> A Song for St. Cecilia's Day, 1687. | Written | By John Dryden, Esq.; and Compos'd by Mr. John Baptist Draghi.

The imprint reads : " Printed by T. Dring, in Fleetstreet, 1687." Draghi's setting has not been published, but copies of the work are preserved in the library of the Royal College of Music, and there is an imperfect copy at the British Museum.

Handel was fifty-four years old when he set the first of Dryden's St. Cecilian odes to music. The autograph score, preserved in the Royal Music Library, Buckingham Palace, bears the following dates :

> Ouverture to the for a Song for at St. Cecilia's Day. ode by Mr. Dryden 1687. Begun Sept. 15. 1739. | ♄
> Fine. G. F. Handel. | Septembr 24. 1739. | ☽

This was the first work in which Handel used the old astrological signs in dating his autograph scores, a custom which he afterwards continued to the end of his life. The manuscript shows some slight though interesting changes. Seven bars of soft music are eliminated from the first movement of the overture ; and the time-signature of " The trumpet's loud clangour " was originally $\frac{3}{8}$. The March is headed " La Marche." At the beginning of the solos Handel has written the names of the principal singers who took part in the first performance—Signora Francesina and Mr. Beard.

The production of the work was advertised in the *London Daily Post and General Advertiser* of November 22, 1739 (St. Cecilia's Day), as follows :

LINCOLNS INN FIELDS.
At the Theatre-Royal in Lincolns Inn Fields, this Day, November 22, (being
St. Cecilia's Day) will be perform'd
An ODE of MR. DRYDEN'S,
With two new CONCERTO's for several Instruments.
Which will be preceded by
ALEXANDER'S FEAST.
And a CONCERTO on the ORGAN.
Boxes Half a Guinea.   Pit 5s.   First Gallery 3s.   Upper Gallery 2s.
. Particular Care has been taken to have the House well-air'd ; and the Passage
from the Fields to the House will be cover'd for better Conveniency.
Box Tickets will be sold this Day at the Stage-Door.

Pit and Gallery Doors will be open'd at Four, the Boxes at Five.
To begin at Six o'Clock.

It will be observed that Handel's name, as composer of the music, does not appear in the above announcement; indeed, in the earliest advertisement, Dryden's name is also suppressed, " A new ode "—not "new" as regards the words—being the only information given as to the identity of the work.   In the advertisement of November 17, the word " warm " appears instead of " well-air'd " in respect of the condition of the " House."

The Ode was performed six times during the winter of 1739-40, in spite of the fact that this was the " hard winter."   The frost lasted nine weeks, when coaches plied upon the Thames, and festivities and diversions of all kinds were enjoyed on the ice-bound river.   No wonder, therefore, that Handel caused the following information to be added to the advertisement (February 13, 1740) of his performances at Lincoln's Inn Theatre :

Particular Care has been taken to have the House survey'd and secur'd against the Cold,
by having Curtains plac'd before every Door, and constant Fires will be kept in the House
'till the Time of Performance.

Although this is the first St. Cecilian ode written by Dryden, it is the second by that poet which Handel set to music.   It was preceded by " Alexander's Feast," composed in 1736.   Mozart wrote, in June, 1790, additional accompaniments to the "Ode on St. Cecilia's Day," as he did to the " Messiah," " Acis and Galatea," and " Alexander's Feast."   Except the " Messiah "—of which the location is unknown—the autographs of Mozart's orchestration of the above works by Handel are preserved in the Royal Library, Berlin.

F. G. E.

AUGUST, 1909.

HANDEL

Ode on St Cecilia's Day

for soprano & tenor soli, SATB & orchestra

words by John Dryden

Order No: NOV 070142

NOVELLO PUBLISHING LIMITED

INDEX.

ODE ON ST. CECILIA'S DAY.

No. 1.

OVERTURE.

HANDEL.

2

No. 2.   RECITATIVE.—"FROM HARMONY."

From har-mo-ny,   from heav'nly har-mo-ny   This u-ni-ver-sal frame be - gan;

No. 8.   RECITATIVE (ACCOMPANIED).—"WHEN NATURE."

No. 4.   Chorus.—" FROM HARMONY."

Handel—Ode on St. Cecilia's Day.   Novello's Edition.   B

8376

Handel—Ode on St. Cecilia's Day. Novello's Edition.   8376

17

in Man. . .

. . in Man. . .

. . in Man. . .

. . in Man. . .

No. 5.   Air.—"WHAT PASSION CANNOT MUSIC RAISE?"

Handel—Ode on St. Cecilia's Day. Novello's Edition.

SOPRANO.

What pas-sion can-not Mu - sic raise and quell?   When

No. 6. Tenor Solo and Chorus—"THE TRUMPET'S LOUD CLANGOUR."

The trumpet's loud clan-gour Ex -

cites us to arms,   ex - cites us to arms,   to

arms, to arms, The trumpets loud clan-gour Ex - cites us to arms,

With shrill notes of .. an - ger And

mor-tal a - larms, ... With shrill notes of anger, with shrill notes of an-ger And

mor-tal a -larms.

The double double double beat Of the thund'ring drum Cries,

Handel—Ode on St. Cecilia's Day. Novello's Edition. C

8376

double double double beat Of the thund'ring drum   Cries, hark! the foe comes; Charge,

charge,   charge,   charge,   charge,   'tis too late, 'tis too late to re-treat,

charge, charge,   charge,   charge, charge, 'tis too late,   too

late to   re-treat.   The trumpet's loud clangour Ex -

CHORUS.

The trumpet's loud clangour Ex - cites us to arms,

The trumpet's loud clangour Ex - cites us to arms,

The trumpet's loud clangour Ex - cites us to arms,

81

No. 7.   MARCH.

No. 8.   Air.—"THE SOFT COMPLAINING FLUTE."

The soft com -

plain - - - - - - ing flute In dy - ing notes dis -
- cov - ers The woes of hope - less
lov - ers, Whose dirge is whis-per'd, whis-per'd,
whis-per'd by the warb - ling lute, by the warb - - -

No. 9.   AIR.—"SHARP VIOLINS PROCLAIM."

42

dame, ... for the fair, dis - dain - ful dame.

Sharp vi - o - lins pro - claim ......

.. Their jeal - ous pangs, their jeal - ous pangs and des - per-

Handel—Ode on St. Cecilia's Day. Novello's Edition.

8376

Handel—Ode on St. Cecilia's Day. Novello's Edition.

8376

No. 10.   AIR (WITH ORGAN OBBLIGATO).—"BUT OH! WHAT ART CAN TEACH."

Adagio.

the choirs a - bove, to mend the choirs a - bove.

Adagio. *a tempo.*

Org. ad lib.

f Str. *p* *f*

tr

No. 11. Air.—"ORPHEUS COULD LEAD THE SAVAGE RACE."

Alla Hornpipe.

f

No. 12.   RECIT. (ACCOMPANIED).—"BUT BRIGHT CECILIA."

But bright Ce - ci-lia rais'd the won-der high'r: When to her or-gan vo-cal breath was giv'n,

An an - gel heard, and straight ap-pear'd Mis-ta-king earth for heaven.

No. 13.   SOLO AND CHORUS.—"AS FROM THE POWER OF SACRED LAYS."

As from the power of sa - cred lays, As from the

53

61

Handel—Ode on St. Cecilia's Day. Novello's Edition.

Printed and bound in Great Britain by
Caligraving Limited Thetford Norfolk

EARLY CHORAL MUSIC

BONONCINI, Antonio
ed Peter Smith
STABAT MATER
For SATB soli, SATB chorus, strings and organ

BONONCINI, Giovanni
ed Anthony Ford
WHEN SAUL WAS KING
For SAT soli, SATB chorus, strings and organ continuo, with optional parts for two oboes and bassoon

GABRIELI, Giovanni
ed Denis Stevens
IN ECCLESIIS
For SATB soli, SATB chorus, instruments and organ

LASSUS, Orlandus
ed Clive Wearing
STABAT MATER
For unaccompanied double choir (SSAT, ATTB)

MONTEVERDI, Claudio
ed John Steele
BEATUS VIR
For SSATTB chorus, instruments and organ continuo

PALESTRINA, da Giovanni
ed W Barclay Squire
STABAT MATER
For unaccompanied double choir (SATB, SATB)

RIGATTI, Giovanni Antonio
ed Jerome Roche
CONFITEBOR TIBI
For SSAATTB chorus, instruments and organ continuo

SCARLATTI, Alessandro
ed John Steele
AUDI FILIA
For SSA soli, SSATB chorus, instruments, string orchestra and organ
ed John Steele
DIXIT DOMINUS
For SATB soli, SATB chorus, strings and organ continuo
ed John Steele
ST CECILIA MASS
For SSATB soli, SATB chorus, strings and organ continuo

VALLS, Francisco
MISSA SCALA ARETINA
For 11 voices in 3 choirs (SAT, SSAT, SATB), orchestra with organ continuo

VARIOUS
TEN RENAISSANCE DIALOGUES
For unaccompanied mixed voices by Lassus, Gabrieli, Morley and others

CHORAL WORKS FOR MIXED VOICES

BACH
CHRISTMAS ORATORIO
For soprano, alto, tenor & bass soli, SATB & orchestra
MASS IN B MINOR
For two sopranos, alto, tenor & bass soli, SSATB & orchestra
ST MATTHEW PASSION
For soprano, alto, tenor & bass soli, SATB & orchestra

BRAHMS
REQUIEM
For soprano & baritone soli, SATB & orchestra

ELGAR
GIVE UNTO THE LORD PSALM 29
For SATB & organ or orchestra

FAURE
ed Desmond Ratcliffe
REQUIEM
For soprano & baritone soli, SATB & orchestra

HANDEL
ed Watkins Shaw
MESSIAH
For soprano, alto, tenor & bass soli, SATB & orchestra

HAYDN
CREATION
For soprano, tenor & bass soli, SATB & orchestra
IMPERIAL 'NELSON' MASS
For soprano, alto, tenor & bass soli, SATB & orchestra
MARIA THERESA MASS
For soprano, alto, tenor & bass soli, SATB & orchestra
MASS IN TIME OF WAR 'PAUKENMESSE'
For soprano, alto, tenor & bass soli,i SATB & orchestra

MONTEVERDI
ed Denis Stevens & John Steele
BEATUS VIR
For soloists, double choir, organ & orchestra
ed John Steele
MAGNIFICAT
For SSATB chorus, instruments & organ
ed Denis Stevens
VESPERS
For soloists, double choir, organ & orchestra

MOZART
REQUIEM MASS
For soprano, alto, tenor & bass soli, SATB & orchestra

SCARLATTI
ed John Steele
DIXIT DOMINUS
For SATB, soli & chorus, string orchestra & organ continuo